# SWEET WISDOMS

# SWEET WISDOMS

Angeline Haen

Shanti Arts Publishing

Brunswick, Maine

SWEET WISDOMS

Published by Shanti Arts Publishing
Designed by Shanti Arts Designs

Shanti Arts LLC
193 Hillside Road
Brunswick, Maine 04011
shantiarts.com

Printed in the United States of America

ISBN: 978-1-941830-48-2 (softcover)
ISBN: 978-1-941830-49-9 (digital)

Library of Congress Control Number: 2017932654

for a Princess and a Buddhist

*Ten times a day something happens to me like this — some strengthening throb of amazement — some good sweet empathic ping and swell. This is the first, the wildest and the wisest thing I know; that the soul exists and is built entirely out of attentiveness.*

— Mary Oliver

# CONTENTS

# PART ONE

# SWEET WISDOMS

## Spiritual Groom

Grooming horses in spring ousts thick flocks of marauding hairs into the air. They penetrate the tightest pursed lips and, by some unknown law, cling in greatest number to the groomer. Coming to the task in the wrong frame of mind, your demeanor can quickly frazzle. After a while, though, the repetitive motion of the curry comb becomes a ritual, and dull thoughts are brushed out with the hair. Gradually, you slip into a meditation, unaware that the horse is reciprocating by grooming your spirit. You look into the horse's relaxed eyes as its head slowly lowers to the ground, and you feel more than winter hair has been shed. Heavy, itchy coats of old patterns are combed through. Knotted strands of thought are loosened from your consciousness. Grooming smooths out your connection with humanity, and your spirit flows freely after you comb through life's tangles.

## STRETCH TO THE LIGHT

Don't you just feel this way sometimes? Our kitty, Glo, had been eating the oxalis plant's new sprouts as soon as they emerged. The plant was struggling but seemed determined to grow, so I moved it to a less conspicuous windowsill. The oxalis' response to my consideration of her predicament was astonishing: in three days she grew four inches. Every white bloom pressed its smiling face against the windowpane, as a baby to its mother's breast, lovingly firm. I imagined their stems extending beyond the pane of glass to embrace the sunbeams themselves.

The oxalis tells us to stretch, to reach for the light, and in turn, the light will reach out to us.

Stretching strengthens our core and gives life flexibility.

Reach beyond your limits, not just to them.

# Good Soup

*It's paradoxical that the idea of living a long life appeals to*
*everyone, but the idea of getting old doesn't appeal to anyone.*
— Andy Rooney

When the white fluffy stuff descends from above with frequent
abundance, I spend more time shoveling than writing. Nothing
goes better with falling snow and temperatures than a
simmering pot of hearty homemade soup accompanied by a
slice of crusty bread for dunking. Chicken and wild rice is on
the menu this day.

I had my yearly checkup today. All is well. I left the clinic
grateful for my good health and that I am growing old. That's
right, I'm thankful for my receding youth. Mind you, I don't feel
I'm aging. Rather, in my forty-eighth winter, I feel I'm growing.

I continue to tweak my recipe for a good life, fortunate to
be afforded the time to simmer, to savor the flavors in the day,
and let them meld into a delicious life. Like a good soup, many
things taste better the next day; sharpness mellows. Sopping
up the day's final spoonfuls becomes an act of self-care. I want
to leave this world with a lasting impression of yum.

## Web Thread

We have but this one strand of aliveness in the web of life. We're not meant to hang on by this thread; we are meant to thread it through the ups and downs, overs and unders, ins and outs; to weave strength into the tapestry of life. Sew your piece of existence into the world.

## Hows and Whys

I've always disliked the word "why." It keeps you stuck. Why can't I find a better job? Why do my relationships fail? Why do these patterns keep repeating? Why is my life so lonely, hard, or boring?

I love the word "how." How can I make things better?

Turn the "whys" into "hows." The responsibility and accountability for the experiences coming into your life are on you. You have to find within yourself the power, courage, and flexibility to change, to get unstuck. What you need will come to you once you decide to make the effort. How do you do it? Begin. Even if at first you're just spinning your wheels, it's still action.

Life's a journey, so move.

# Free Music

Before rousing in the morning, there is a hole in time when you slip out of and into slumber; a tug-of-war takes place between your brain and body to decide which will prevail: sleep or wakefulness. I was once in this dreamy paradise when a sudden feeling of panic charged through me. I popped up in bed feeling something was awry. Instinctively, I looked out my bedroom window toward the horse shelter. Duchess seemed occupied with something out of my view. The seventeen-year-old pinto mare is the sentry in our little herd of three.

Then I saw what I was feeling: Jazz was trotting around outside the electric fence with a very high opinion of himself for escaping his man-made boundaries. He does this on occasion: slips under the fence to get out and then slips under the fence to get back in. The five-year-old Mini-Appaloosa is the live wire in the herd. He has an innate ability to sense a disabled shocker. On this occasion it was grounded by a snowbank. While plowing out snow around the barn, my son had pushed it into the lower wire, causing the fence to ground. This means there is no shock administered when an animal touches it.

Jazz can get into all kinds of mischief in the summer, but winter? Eh, no harm done. One reason of many to love this little rogue pony is his "all up in your face" pony attitude.

Another is that I also have days when I can't be fenced in. Jazz plays a wild soul groove. Our relationship is interplayed with unpredictable improvisation, atonal forays of free Jazz I've come to enjoy. As long as the rest of the band stays in the fence, we're good!

## Soil to Soul

A good part of Saturday was spent preparing and planting a new grass pasture for the horses. Anyone who works the land knows proper seedbed preparation is essential to good seed germination. Machinery tills the soil until it is loose and smooth. Newly seeded land looks wide open, naked, and as vulnerable as a baby. Yet, it holds on to its dignity. I am reminded how vulnerability brings compassion alive.

Whatever seeds you want to sow in your life — forgiveness, love, peace, joy, contentment, abundance, tolerance — they grow best in a good soul foundation. Cultivating a spiritually rich life begins with a well prepared soulbed. Like soil, our souls are full of potential to grow. Let us prepare ourselves so we might be the green pastures in the life we grow for our children.

# Waiting on Rain

We'd been waiting for weeks for the rain to come to northern Wisconsin. Then, one day plump droplets arrived. Descending from a sky stroked with wide swaths of gray, I heard the steady slow measures — a farmer's rain, as they say. I was delighted to wake up the next day and find we were still enjoying the rain's company!

There are times when rain can be an annoyance, dropping by unexpectedly or overstaying its welcome, but even during these times, you shouldn't curse the rain. Somewhere, someone is praying for rain.

Listening to rain, our emotions swell and ping. Downpours wash over and away, like a cleansing gush over our emotional body. It's in the presence of these gentle rains that I am called to soak in stillness and listen for the ping.

# Honey Flow

The seasons have once again circled around to the time
of honey harvest. For months, in their inner sanctuary of
complete darkness, the bees have collaborated with the hive's
mother — the Queen — to create what shines in the absence
of light: a golden heart of honey!

The bees strum the flowers' fragrance into song. Through
the air their sweet buzz vibrates. Bees remind us that there is
an abundance of nectar running through life. Your heart is your
hive, a sanctuary that stores life's honey flow. If you don't swat,
you can taste it without getting stung.

# Dad's Hanky

I'm thinking about my Dad's red hanky today. Now-a-days, people call the hanky a bandanna. It's a hanky. He always had one peeking out from his back pants pocket. He'd use two fingers to tuck it deep inside, but a dog-ear of red always managed to hang over the pocket opening's hem. Dad had huge "cucumber" fingers from years of physical work on and off the farm. I don't think he could get more than two fingers to fit in a pocket at one time.

Dad never left the house without three things: his cigarettes, jackknife, and a paisley-print hanky. The faithful hanky wiped off sweat and boogers, soaked up blood and tears. I saw it used as a muzzle, headband, Band-Aid, tourniquet, flag, grease rag, hair tie, land marker, hot pad, dust mask, scarf, an object for a spur-of-the-moment game of peek-a-boo or tug-of-war, and oh so much more I've forgotten.

The same hanky stayed in his pocket most of a week, being used over and over again until wash day on Saturday. Still, whether it was Sunday or Friday, we never gave a second thought to using it.

The hankies were neatly ironed and folded in a perfect square then placed in the bedroom dresser, middle drawer, right front corner. I never could understand why Mom ironed them because the crisp folds rumpled at the first tuck. I'd say it was Mom's way of showing Dad she cared, and that would be reason enough.

Red was the preferred color, but a few blue ones rounded out the dozen or so in waiting. When Dad asked me to retrieve a hanky from the drawer, I'd ransack the neat piles until I found an old faded one. They were especially soft and pliable. The torn corners bore witness to their long life and added an extra dimension of fun to an easily distracted child like myself, should I happen to be in need of a hanky, the need being real or imagined.

Hankies could become so many things when put in the hands of a child. I kept one of Dad's hankies after he crossed over into Spirit. Now and again, I pull out the hanky I saved and bury my nose deep in the fragrance of fond childhood memories permeating the fabric. Even in heaven, there is no doubt Dad has a hanky at the ready in case I have a hurt to wipe away or soak up. Invisible hankies from heaven, folded and tucked into my heart.

## Bare Soles

*I want to be where your bare foot walks, because maybe before*
*you step, you'll look at the ground. I want that blessing.* — Rumi

I live in bare feet, delighting in my wiggly toes free of fancy.
Dark soil is packed tight under my toenails from April
to September. The soles of my feet take on a seasonal
stain of earthy brown tones. The stain defines the delicate,
permanently etched heel cracks in my callused skin, giving
them the appearance of an ancient script scrolled into their
perimeter. I believe there is some primal, immortal soul
language spoken between bare feet and Mother Earth, an
energetic conversation with an uninhibited flow. Bare your
soles! Walk in the naked truth of beauty's bareness. Match
your footsteps to Mother Earth's heartbeat, and this earth walk
you're on becomes a soul conversation.

# Florence

Florence our cat has a meow that sounds like she's a two-pack-a-day smoker. It's unbecoming to the feminine energy that pulses from every hair on her body. Her hips move with such grace, Marilyn Monroe would be envious! And that long, soft hair and those sensual green eyes. She is all lady! She hunts all night and returns without so much as a smudge on her brilliant white coat!

Ms. Florence is the second cat we've received serendipitously, a stray in the bus yard. She left a gift of rodent on the front stoop one day that I am willing to say must have come from the neighbor's yard. It was huge! Dare I say near rat size? We have learned to make our first steps out the door well-placed and light lest we feel the dreaded ooze of a mouse corpse press against the sole of a shoe or, in my case, foot — I go barefoot all the time.

These frequent gifts mean each day starts with rodent funeral duty. Some days the rodents are given an informal funeral, a quick flick of the shovel, and other times a proper burial beneath the earth, always with a few words of gratitude for their sacrifice, and the nourishment they provided for Flo. By the sway of her belly and the look of satisfaction on her face, she eats her fill. Still, I don't like to see anything die without purpose and honor. So today I hope to devise a platform of some sort to offer up the gifts as a snack for a passing hawk or crow. Flo's abundant feminine energy is probably what makes her such a good huntress; she has a relentless drive to provide.

Throughout life our teachers come in limitless forms and ways. The best come serendipitously.

# Ear Mittens

*Love is the only prayer I know.*
— Marion Zimmer Bradley, *The Mists of Avalon*

When Lakota, our seven-year-old gelding, came to us from a horse rescue, it was apparent that he had suffered frostbite on his ear. The tip was permanently bent backwards at a ninety-degree angle, and most of the ear lacked hair. During the summer months, I watched it for signs of sunburn. The ear did fine. I decided to sew an "ear mitten" for him before the arrival of winter.

Tape measure in hand, I headed out to the pasture one day. I also carried with me a pad of paper and pen. I didn't have a design plan, and it turned out I didn't need one. A miracle had occurred over the summer, and I hadn't even noticed: the once naked ear was covered with hair! Could it be that by creating a miracle, we allow the unexpected to happen miraculously?

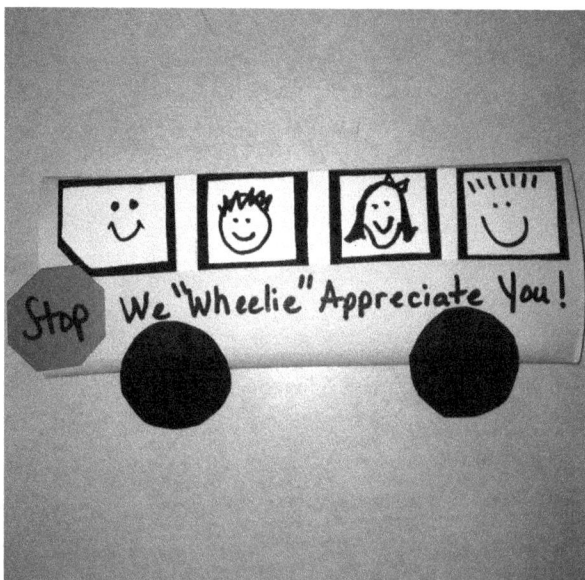

# PART TWO

# FOUR YEARS WISE

# Ears and Eyes

This year's batch of four-year-old kindergärtners on the school van I drive have an overwhelming case of ants in their pants. They are fascinated with standing on the seats and jumping from seat to seat. They are like popcorn kernels in a pot of hot oil. The teachers and I have been working on reinforcing "bottoms touching the seat" and "hands to yourself."

One of the boys — Boy #1 — figured out I can watch them with my mirror, and he tried to explain this to his friend — Boy #2:

Boy #1: "She gotz a mirror she looks in."

Boy #2: "That's for cars, not us."

Boy #1: "No, watch her. See! There! Did you see her?"

I'm smiling at this point. Both quickly duck behind the seats. This back and forth continues until I gently remind them of the rules. Mind you, the conversation they are having is very loud. I guess they are so focused on my seeing them, they forget I can also hear them!

## Swallowed Soul

"I know how to get undead," he says excitedly. "I know how to get undead!" he repeats in a near shout. "First, you need a soul. I have one!"

Now he's got my attention. My eyes are on the road and my hands are on the steering wheel, but my ears are at a ninety-degree bend listening to the chirping four-year-old sitting three seats back.

"It can talk to you too!" he adds.

I'm impressed.

"I know where it lives," he continues on as his captivated audience of peers fires several rounds of questions at him: "How did you find it? Is it far away? What's a soul ?"

The questions suddenly cease and a hush comes over the van as the little boy announces, "Watch out, I'm gonna show you where!"

I'm welling up with joy. How wonderful that a four-year-old understands to follow his heart. I wait for his answer, glancing every few seconds to catch the obvious: his little hands folded over his heart.

"It's right here, right here . . . in your neck!" He grabs a pinch of skin on his neck and stretches it out from his throat, wiggling it back and forth for emphasis.

I manage to hold back an outburst of laughter, but a short giggle-snort escapes nonetheless. Choking the burst of laughter, I can't help thinking that I may have swallowed my soul!

## Dad's Eyes

I have a new four-year-old kindergärtner who recently rode with me for the first time. The paperwork states he is a Special Ed student. He is a pure delight. The first thing he said as his dad buckled him in was, "What's your name?"

"I'm Angie," I replied.

"You're my bus driver," he shouted and off we went. A bit later he said, "This isn't the way to school."

"We have to pick up more friends first, and then we go to school," I replied.

"Oh, more friends are coming, everyone! More friends are coming!" he sang out. He then asked me to take off my sunglasses. I did.

"Can you look at me?" he asked. I did.

He then said, "Your eyes are blue, a pretty blue like your dad's, but he's not here. My eyes are green like my dad's, but he's here."

Oh, I'd say he's special alright. I like to think my Dad had a little something to do with this "special" delivery message.

## Do Some Good

One of my kindergärtners was quite upset when I picked her up one day because she hadn't had time to brush her teeth after eating lunch. Her mommy told her she is supposed to brush her teeth before school. I said, "Well, if you brush your teeth more times than not, it'll do some good, which is better than no good." At this I got a smile, closely chased by a giggle indicating her approval.

I wondered how I could apply this lesson to my own life. If I could be more understanding, more kind, more open, and more patient more times than not, I would be doing some good, which is better than no good.

The action of doing is what instills in us the desire to do more. Meaning is created by doing. When your actions speak, you need no words to explain.

# Pee In a Pod

One day during my afternoon kindergärtner route, a little girl
came up to my seat. She shaped her chubby little index finger
into a hook and with it motioned for me to come closer. I
leaned in as she whispered, "Bus driver, I have to go pee, really,
really, really bad!"

I reply, "Let's have you sit tight right here, and I mean tight.
Squeeze your legs together as tight as you can, okay? You can
even squeeze your eyes if that helps," I tell her.

At this I get a nod. I then radio in, "Van sixty-three has a
leg-crosser, ten minutes out. Have a teacher at the door." In
the movie *Monsters, Inc.*, there is a frantic scene where there's
"human contamination." Buzzers and bells go off. Workers
with hazmat suits swarm to the sight. Chaos ensues until the
contamination is contained. Well, that just about sums up what
I would go through if bodily fluids left little bodies and got on
my bus.

Two minutes from school I look over to check on her and
see that a friend is helping squeeze her legs together at the
knees while another is holding her eyes shut. Both friends also
have their eyes squeezed shut. We not only need the help of
our friends to get by, we also need their help at times to hold
us together.

# Butt Driver

*If the world appears abundant in smiles or overwhelmed by*
*scowls, you might ask yourself if you're not to blame.*
— Richelle E. Goodrich, *Smile Anyway*

In my ten years of driving a school bus, I have found there
are inevitably certain topics of conversation that are sure to
pop up each year among the little riders. One of these is
a discussion of poop and pee. I generally give the children
freedom to share their limited understanding and stories about
peeing behind a tree while camping or off the boat while fishing
with Grandpa.

A little girl once approached and told me that so-and-so
(the name shall remain anonymous) called me a "butt driver."

I gasped. Her eyes opened as large as a full moon, and she
said with conviction, "I herds it with my own ears!"

When we reached the school, I let all the kids exit, but
motioned for "so-and-so" to come to me. I said to this
child, "I hear you called me a butt driver." I'm sure his words
were meant to be more playful than hurtful, but this is still a
teachable moment. "If I'm a butt driver, what does that make
you?" I ask him.

Without missing a beat, he replied, "A little shit."

Well, I was thinking "stinker," but I'm not going to argue a moot point. I assured him our words were between me, him, and the fence post, and I went on to explain that once words come out, you can't put them back in. We shared a giggle when I tried my best to explain the term "diarrhea of the mouth," the point being that it's okay to have nothing to say, which is much better than saying something you will later regret.

After some contemplation, I realized that I can't change words spoken by someone else, but I can change the energy with which I receive them. Words have a boomerang effect; the trick is to respond rather than react. If I had "reacted," my words would have been said in a mean-spirited way. They would have been terse and unyielding. By "responding" instead of "reacting," the words I returned to him carried understanding, not meanness.

Thus we parted in good spirits and as friends.

For me, the big picture is the relationship we have with all that surrounds us. If we happen to throw a few boomerangs, may they return to us in good way.

## Alarming Fire

I was driving along when I heard a loud voice yell, "It's on fire! Put it out. Put it out! Your hat's on fire!"

What? I take a peek in my mirror. Behind the seats, little heads started popping out into the aisle. A moment passed, then, "We're not kidding. It's on fire. Hurry! Put it out!"

What?!! This warrants further investigation. I pulled over, undid my seatbelt, and spun around. The four-year-olds' faces were stone-gray. All I heard was breathing as I walked to the back of the van. Then I saw the "fire." It was a huge red hat topper, bouncing on a wee girl's head. I pierced the quiet with a loud thunder of words. "What are you all standing around for? You, grab that bucket. You, the hose."

The kids didn't waste a pinch of time getting into the playful impromptu skit. I let their youthful energy burn out with the announcement that it began to rain. It was time to douse the flames of excitement before it turned into a wildfire.

"Whew!" Cheers, giggles, and claps filled the air. Imaginations fully engaged, I pulled back onto the road.

A tiny spark of imagination had this van full of four-year-olds on fire. The creative spirit is stoked by imagination's inextinguishable aliveness, and there is nothing more alive than a van full of four-year-olds with their imaginations on fire!

## SILENT SONG

One afternoon the four-year-old kindergärtners I drive to
school had their Christmas program. I hardly recognized one
of the little boys when he got on the van; he was all shined up,
and I told him so. He responded, "Mama had to put lots of
water on my hair to get it to look like this, and I have really nice,
really nice clothes on under my jacket." As he spoke these
words he poked his puffed-out chest.

In the van, the children spontaneously began to sing their
program songs for me. I keyed my two-way radio so the entire
fleet could hear. One of the male drivers came on the radio
with a hearty "Ho, Ho, Ho!" and pure joy swirled around inside
the vehicle. I loved how everyone got swept away with the
spirit of the season.

Then the children sang a song I had never heard before.
One of the little girls said, "Well, we've heard it lots! Over and
over and over," she paused to gasp for air, "and over and over
again!"

I was certain they were all warmed up for their
performance. I left them with one bit of advice: "Remember
that the best way to spread Christmas cheer is to sing loudly
for all to hear!" And so they did . . . off the bus, down the
sidewalk, past the teacher, and into the school. I was confused

by the teacher's panicked hand gestures to quiet them down. How could she not be in the holiday spirit on this, the last day before Christmas break? Then I realized that the toddlers in daycare across the hall from the kindergarten classroom were napping. Oops!

The best way to spread Christmas cheer is to quietly let our hearts sing the whole year through.

# God Has Answered

*It's the action, not the fruit of the action, that's important. You have to do the right thing. It may not be in your power, may not be in your time, that there will be any fruit. But that doesn't mean you stop doing the right thing. You may never know what results come from your action. But if you do nothing, there will be no result.* — Mahatma Gandhi

I was on duty to be second advocate at the Sexual Assault Center (SAC) one night, but I got a call at 5:30 telling me to go to St. Vincent's. Apparently, there had been a sexual assault on a two-year-old, and the first volunteer couldn't be reached.

I became quite upset, nearly angry, so on the drive in I decided to do some peeling.

I was in the middle of making a cake for my mother-in-law's birthday, but I am free all day tomorrow. Peel that back. It was cold outside, and I'd been in and out of the cold all day. Peel that back.

I wasn't in the mood to deal with the ugly side of human beings right then. Besides, I was starting to feel that I don't make a difference anyway. What I didn't know was that this call-out was about to prove my thinking wrong. It was going to show me that the other side of ugly is beautiful.

So what is it? How come the anger lingered? Could it be that I don't feel I'm making a difference? Bingo! In this work, we do lots of information-gathering, paperwork, and sibling-sitting, but I'm not sure I "touch" people. It's strange to feel this because the officers and hospital staff are always expressing their appreciation for the volunteers. I peeled this back and scratched at the next layer. I asked my guides, guardians, ancestors, and the Creator to give me proof that I am making a difference in the lives of sexual assault victims. I'm looking for answers. Help me overcome my doubt.

I arrived at the hospital and sat with the sister while Mom was in a room with her two-year-old daughter who was being examined by a sexual assault nurse. I brought out my stock of markers, paper, and stickers. The sister and I decided to draw and color a garden.

I'm a so-so artist, but to this four-year-old, I was Picasso! As we finished she said, "This is the most beautiful drawing ever! Is it okay if I put a heart sticker on it? Because I love you. I love love love you!"

As I held back tears, she asked if she could have the drawing. I gave it to her, and she reciprocated by giving me her precious Hello Kitty sticker. "This is for you," she told me.

When I arrived home, I had the urge to find the meaning of her name. I did a little research and found it; it means "God has answered."

Never doubt that you make a difference; never doubt the blessing that your life is to this world.

# PART THREE

# NATURE'S TONGUE

## BOWL OF COLD

Crunchy invigoration is vibrating through the entirety of my being after walking Wally , our yellow Labrador Retriever, on this crisp morning. I'm starting my day with the goodness of natural nourishment; I grabbed a bowl of cold and spooned it in! The voice of the snow with each crunchy, crusty footstep snapped me awake. Starting out frozen fresh has me hot-n-ready for the day ahead.

## CHIMES

I was gifted a Woodstock wind chime tuned to the song "Amazing Grace." The strong wind today is playing the sweetest melody. I can hear it inside our home. The beautiful enchanting music is causing me to pause and listen, pause and listen, as I work. I believe the chime has charmed the voices of the celestial world into song here on earth.

# INDIAN PIPE

I made a discovery! An Indian Pipe plant, also known
as a Ghost Flower, is growing in the woods under a few
chokecherry trees. I immediately knew what this plant was
because it's pictured on the cover of one of my medicinal herb
books.

Indian Pipe is translucent white, "naked," meaning it
produces no chlorophyll. It's actually a parasite that feeds on
both decaying forest vegetation and living trees. By tapping
into the relationship between trees and fungi, the Indian Pipe
gets a free ride. It doesn't have to produce carbohydrates or
find minerals to live.

This is what I find so fascinating about nature. Hidden
within its infinite wonder are intriguing oddballs, plants like the
Ghost Flower that create their own unique way of being in this
world. Every excursion into the vast diversity of nature is an
invitation to nurture our curiosity and appeal to the wisdom of
knowing we all choose how we live.

## FLOAT

Heaven's voice is preaching to the sky. Life is awakened within me as an impending storm gathers strength. Beneath me, the ground momentarily vibrates from a thunder's boom, and the wind rushes answers to waiting prayers below.

As a child, thunderstorms were sermons on fear. It took some life experience and a higher perspective to view them differently. Refuge came by surrendering to the struggle. I let go of control and allowed myself to float into the clouds of fear. I learned to wallow in the trust of a higher power.

Storms continue to thunder their sermons of fear across the sky, but I'm no longer in the congregation. I'm floating on faith, watching fear blow by.

## CRUEL COLD

Here in Wisconsin, it's freeze- your-nose-hairs-together and turn-your-whiskers-frosty kind of weather. As I make my morning round of chores, I keep pulling my hat down and my long underwear up! You can feel the landscape's bones on these sharp cold days. I delight in the simplicity of winter — stay warm. Bitter cruel cold, you can't make me a bitter, cruel cold person!

## Beginning Fields

Tractor fumes mingle with the sweet scent of freshly turned hay. The sickle cut close to the earth. Tall proud stems and blades laid down and dried by the breath of the sun. A steady parade of bulging squares marched out of the baler to be stacked in an orderly fashion on the hayrack, and following each, a cough of fine chafe that stuck to beads of sweat draped across my brow. Bald fields void of lush green begin again.

When the daylight is extinguished I'll rest, my forearms speckled with tiny cuts from the stiff stems of hay, my fingers swollen from plucking taut twine. To know that this labor keeps hunger from winter's long reach and squeezes the throat of drought gives my soul temporary satisfaction.

Next summer, I'll begin again like green fields.

# Eye On The Sparrow

It is early afternoon, and the bus yard has settled into the lull between routes. I'm making my way along the railing to my school bus, number 169, when something catches my eye. It's a sparrow, hovering in front of another bus's windshield. I pause and give my full attention to the little sparrow's activity. The drab plumage and familiarity of Sparrows permits them to generally go about their business unnoticed. At times, it rests on the edge of a wiper blade, head tense and twisted. Charged with enthusiasm, the little Sparrow feasts on bug bodies and separated parts stuck to the windshield. Down the line it moves to the next bus, expanding its free buffet to bus grills and the backs of both rear view mirrors. In the future, we may want to rethink using the phrase "bird brain" when referring to the dimwitted!

There is something else about this little bird. As I watch and listen, it displays dignity and a sense of worthiness in the easy meal, endlessly chipping in delight. The Sparrow loves life as much as life loves the Sparrow. No matter how insignificant we believe his lot of existence to be, the Sparrow thrives on surviving. In the soul-stirring gospel hymn, "His Eye Is on the Sparrow," there is a lyric that goes, "God has his eye on the sparrow and I know he watches over me." I felt God's eyes on me while I imagined him with his eye on the Sparrow.

# Unclouded Day

*What sunshine is to flowers, smiles are to humanity. These are but trifles, to be sure; but scattered along life's pathway, the good they do is inconceivable.* — Joseph Addison

A kiss to this unclouded day! It felt good to be out in the sunshine and I am thankful for the way the sun's warm spirit washed over and through me, scrubbing clean the stubborn darkness between my ears. That's the kind of light to shine — the natural warm glow that comes from a person's sunspot, their heart, not a glaring cold florescent mind. Pass along love's warm glow with a sunshine smile to uncloud someone's day. Turn your sunspot on the world. Be someones sunshine.

# WHITE PINE BRANCH

*Being happy doesn't mean that everything is perfect. It means
that you've accepted that life isn't perfect but you're experiencing
all of it with gusto anyway! You'll screw up. You'll fall down.
We all do. But that doesn't need to stop you from embracing
life with wide open arms and an open heart.* — Denise Linn,
internationally respected healer, writer, and teacher

During a late January storm, the landscape was covered with
ten inches of heavy wet snow. Walking our property line shortly
afterwards, I noticed a large branch of a White Pine tree broke
from the weighty snow burden. The limb bent at a sharp
angle about eight feet from where it grew out of the tree. The
inside wood was splintered and protruded from the outer bark,
criss-crossing at the place that still anchored the branch to the
trunk. Bowed to the ground, the end of the branch seemed to
be kissing the earth goodbye. Andy wanted to cut it off, but I
told him to wait until the needles turn brown. We decided to
wait. The proud tree stood with several sisters flanking each side.
Together they formed a living fence between our property and
the neighbor's.

The weeks turned into months. The months became years. It's
close to seven now, yet not a single needle has a mention of brown. I

stop often to admire this humble pine and its almost broken branch.

A few years back after hunting season, a doe hobbled into the side field. Four inches was shot off one of her front legs, and a thin strip of hide kept the dangling leg attached. I begged Andy to shoot her, to please put her out of her misery. He told me he couldn't because of the laws of the Department of Natural Resources (DNR) and then went on to explain the resiliency of whitetail deer. I fumed over his reluctance and kept the deer close in thought and prayer throughout the winter. I was pleasantly surprised when the doe returned to our side field in the spring looking robust and in good spirit. The surprise turned into shock when we saw she was accompanied by a wobbly newborn fawn. When she grazed or walked, the shorter front leg was used like a crutch to support her weight. Running was more of a hop on three legs. The second summer we were elated to spy twins following her out of the woods.

She did more than survive.

The pine and the doe taught me that sometimes we rush to an ending we've predetermined. In unpredictable ways, new beginnings emerge and grow into a new life. Often we hurry to alter the course of things, missing the perfection in imperfection, the wholeness. I held the expectation of death for both the pine branch and the doe. Instead, they held the intention of resurrection.

If you can get beyond your brokenness, you will heal.

## Winter Weeps

Winter's tenacious grip on the landscape is easing with each soft plink-plink-plop sound that drips inside my ear. I hear winter weeping. Cold water droplets tenderly caress the dagger-like icicles clenched to the eaves. March's growling lion is quieted by the warmth of the sunbeam's closeness. The fangs of the weakened white beast jut from the roof's edge, dribbling with the mouth-watering anticipation of spring. It's not the pang of anger but the ache of longing that draws drool. Winter weeps not for its passing, but the lingering wait for spring's embrace.

## Spring's Promise

The crippling winter is leaning hard on the crutch of spring. Each day, I watch them hobble slowly past, yoked together by the same forces that want to pull them apart. I find comfort in knowing summer will heal all that winter has broken, even the promise of an early spring.

## Between Breaths

I'm relaxed and recharged after a week on the river with family.
There was an active eagle's nest across the lake from the
cottage we rented. The pair came almost daily to fish in our
cove, catching a Northern Pike one morning that we estimated
was over twenty inches long. The lake carried their voices to us.
One felt their excitement when feeding their young and their
tension when the crows came too close to the nest. Nature
has a way of showing us how quickly life comes and goes. Yet
there is a peace in knowing one feeds the other. Emptiness is
filled. Fullness is emptied. We're living and dying in the same
breath. Make the inhales fully alive and the exhales fully empty.
In between, life happens.

Live there.

# SOAK

*The secret of patience is doing something else in the meanwhile.*
— Unknown

I heard the soft swollen drops of spring dancing on the roof, and I felt their music: a slow waltz. Their dinging tapped out a mocking laugh directed at the lengthy list of outdoor tasks I had compiled for the day. The winter past held teachings of endurance. This spring, it's the wisdom of measured patience.

I've noticed the elderberry and apple tree leaves are now open after being held tight in bud for the last few weeks. The divine patience of the Creator can be seen everywhere in nature.

The list is set aside for the meantime, and I decide to busy myself with creating a large pot of split-pea soup. Reading through the recipe I realize I need to let the hard dry peas soak for an hour and wonder if anything is going to get accomplished before dark.

I wait patiently for time to swell and soften the soaking split-peas. I need something to do until the rain subsides and the peas have increased in size. In the meantime, I stand in the mind's classroom, a willing pupil eager to learn the quality of patience.

## PRUNED LIFE

There was a time when I walked anxiously around and around each apple tree, studying the tree from every possible angle, trying to decide which branch to prune. I knew the benefits, but the task was filled with angst and indecision. All of that changed after I took a pruning class a few years back. I now enjoy the late winter pruning of our apple orchard.

I was taught there are three reasons to prune: to maintain structure, to provide light channels, and to improve air flow. When in doubt cut it out. Pruning keeps the tree balanced.

Three reasons to prune your life: maintain structure, provide light channels, and allow for flow. Pruning keeps us balanced. When in doubt, cut it out! It's a good time to sharpen your shears and let things go.

# PART FOUR

# WALKING WALLY

## Unfettered Joy

Wally turns his head towards the creek. Nose in the lead, tilted skyward. His dense yellow fur resembles fish scales after jumping into the creek on our first pass through the area, but waterlogged fur coats are never a burden to yellow labs. The wind has died. Wally trots past two preening chickadees perched low on a birch branch; a male and female, I presume. Wally pauses briefly to vacuum the trunk with his nose. The stillness erupts with a flurry of calls. *Chicka dee-dee-dee-dee-dee. Chicka dee-dee-dee-dee.* The playful giggle of water in the background hushes as if to listen. In an instant, the masked pair dart through a matrix of branches and land safe and settled on the bounciest top limbs. Feathers shake from beak to toe. Fluffy calm is regained.

On the right, we pass a forgotten rock pile gathered over decades from the surrounding farm fields. Grapevines and blackberry stems camouflage their existence. No longer polished by the open hand of the elements, thick mats of moss and fungi lay on their faces like overdone make-up. In a gap, no bigger than the width of my thumb, I see a forked tongue flicker, wildly flapping up and down, in and out. Then Wally sees what I see. Without hesitation, he jams his nose, which is substantially larger than the width of my thumb, into the gap. Distorting his nose as he tries to twist and turn it into the small opening. He retreats to sneeze, undeterred, and his paw swipes at the opening. Rocks big and small tumble. I leave them where they come to rest.

Straight ahead, an elbow sharp bend turns the creek north. Here there is mercy: soft sand, a deep quiet pool. Before and after there is a raw edge where flowing water meets standing land. Exposed roots dangle helplessly above the water's surface in this hollow space.

Further down, the cool water slaps at a long-fallen log. A good six inches in diameter, half its length is beneath the flow and its skin is absent. Wally somehow sees an indiscernible turtle straddling the dark smooth log. Neck fully extended, eyes folded closed.

Wally jumps, all fours clear the ground and with a marvelous splash he lands. Head plunges beneath the water surface to his eyes. Then his head pops up, and down again to his ears. Then up and down again, blowing water bubbles and hacking after each failed attempt to catch the turtle. Then, at the far bank, he hears the sound of a frog plopping into the water. Wally jumps, again all fours clear the ground and with a marvelous splash he lands. His head plunges below the surface of the water, and once again, he bobs up and down, blowing bubbles and hacking up swallowed water, but the frog escapes.

Tongue lolled to one side of his mouth, Wally momentarily waits for his breathing to slow. Then with an "all at once" hop, he lands on the bank. Ears stiff and square. Eyes sharp and tight. Nostrils open and alert, a final scan is taken. Water streams down his sides as he rolls his saturated coat from side to side in great yellow waves, nearly tipping himself over. His blue bone-shaped name tag dingles and jingles. Satisfied that he is less wet and I am less dry, we head the long way home while I think out loud that we must keep company with the creek more often.

# WALKING FENCE LINES

Walking Wally this morning, we stuck to the fence line. The edge of the tamed field is overgrown with brambles, vines, scraggly trees, and thickets of thorny shrubs. Wally loves weaving in and out, chasing the scent of unseen things. The unkempt space teems with hidden aliveness.

We all have fence lines in our lives, those tangled spaces we let overgrow to the point we can't walk through so we walk away or around. Still, there may come a time when it is necessary to cross those fence lines, examine every old post, twig, and stone until we find a way through. In the course of weaving in and out, we learn the value of obstacles. We learn how far we can go if we don't let anything stop us.

# First Snow

*Kindness is like snow — it beautifies everything it covers.*
— Kahlil Gibran

The Creator covered Mother Earth with winter's white cloak last night. Some flakes were still on their descent, gracefully floating down to their patiently waiting mother as Wally and I began our walk this morning.

Wally could not contain his giddiness. Nor could I! How can you not feel the mystical magic of the cosmos in the season's first snowfall? All of the world's hardness softens. What a good morning to pause and infuse one's spirit with pure white magic. Then you can use your shovel wand to make the snow disappear from your driveway!

# Little Trails

There is a little trail along the edge of the prairie that we occasionally use as a shortcut to the back field. I've been walking the worn, slightly sloping, ambling path for twenty-some odd years. It hugs the tree line and kisses the lip of wild grasses that stretch to the tree line far in the distance. It is a betwixt and between place, filling its visitors with spirited vigor.

I have kept company with two- and four-leggeds on this trail. They have left their footprints on my heart, delightful energetic impressions tenderly pressed into the earth by beautiful souls. Time has worn a path, a shortcut, to the love that connects us.

This morning I am reminded to walk gently in this life, or walk away. Be mindful where you place your steps when you walk into another's heart.

## Catch Joy

I used to think Wally's one-track mind didn't serve him very well. He has missed countless rabbits, chippys, and squirrels because of his insistence that they were hunkered down in the brush pile. Of course, they had long since scampered away and were halfway across the woods while he was running himself dizzy around the brush pile.

My viewpoint has changed, though, after seeing the complete state of bliss Wally can spin himself into by chasing after life. He has taught me that you don't have to "catch" something to find joy. You can also find it by chasing it. Indeed you might never catch it, but what a blast you can have just smelling around for it.

## Wonder Full Life

Our cat, Glo, accompanied Wally and me on our wonder-filled walk this morning. It generally takes us thirty minutes, depending on how long we stop to wonder. Wally wondered if the vole was still in his hole, and Glo wondered how much more there was to explore.

Wonder is the place our capacity to notice life increases. It's where imagining possibilities manifests into insights. There is knowing in not knowing. It starts with you being wonder full.

## Peace Walk

Over the years, walking Wally has become a prayer; each footstep bestowing a wish to Mother Earth, each breath bestowing a hope to the Father Sky. Every unspoken word carried to the heavens like an ancestral echo one hears in the heart, and every beat a ripple of sacred motion. There is peace here in this world. Some days I find it. Some days I make it.

# Winter Waddle

It seems Wally can't differentiate between a balmy eighty degrees and a frigid ten below. The weather conditions bear no weight in his decision to walk or not walk. His enthusiasm is unwavering. Given that I value my sanity, walk we must!

Over the years, we have faced nature's raw elements together. I have expanded my collection of outdoor apparel over time with the intention of being prepared for all types of weather occasions. The "collection" I have amassed includes several pairs of hi-tech long underwear, assorted wool socks and hats, rain gear worthy of a duck's jealousy, and heavily insulated boots and gloves.

As usual, by the time we turn for home, I'm so hot that I'm carrying more clothes than I'm wearing. Growing up, I was taught that when it's cold outside, you need to wear layers. If movement is difficult and you are uncomfortable, you have on sufficient insulation to stave off death by freezing. I have come to realize, however, that I believe I have to bundle up to stay warm and safe in other ways. Layers are protection against the cold, but also against certain people and experiences, which means I waddle uncomfortably through life.

It's time to unbundle layers of uncomfortable core beliefs that no longer fit who I am. It's time to move freely into my authentic self, picking through my layers of perspectives and choosing the ones that don't make me too hot or too cold. I want the perspectives that make me feel just right.

## Think Shine Not Whine

I saw a beautiful sun dog lazily dangling a rainbow-hued leg above me in the sky this afternoon. The brightly colored patch of light hovered next to the sun. Wally and I both needed to squint when the sun's smile faced us. The snow's icy glare turned the strands of sunlight into tiny bright sparks that danced upon the cold earth, like their cousins in the night sky, but these stars frolicked beneath our feet, and the open field transformed into a cosmic dance floor.

Winter's song is silent to our ears but is heard with one's heart, that is, unless we beat it to death with the drum of our constant complaining. Winter's song comes from deep in the throat of stillness. From this place of tranquility, silence says everything words cannot.

Reflect. Listen with your heart. Allow the twinkles of cold to freshen the staleness in your discontent with winter. Think shine, not whine! This winter season, I hope you hear the music to winter's song and get out on the dance floor.

# Best Dog-Christmas Ever

Christmas came a day late for Wally this year, but the intention of the gift, a pleasant walk in the woods, took several unexpected turns.

My son Peter and I took Wally for a five-mile hike through the big woods. The first surprise, which shouldn't have surprised us at all, was our encounter with a putrid, unidentifiable substance that perfumed the immediate area with a burn-your-nose-hairs stench, and we were barely a mile down the trail. Wally could not believe his good fortune and immediately rolled his body in the foul-smelling pile.

Surprise number two was a new four-legged friend that sparked Wally's seldom-seen frisky side. This was a nice departure from the serious pursuit of unique scents and wild things. His new friend must have thought that any dog that smells that awful has to be awesome!

The pinnacle of Wally's woodsy walk came shortly after we climbed the last hill for home; it took the form of a decomposing deer carcass. We had difficulty persuading Wally to leave the delicacy. On his insistence, a portion of the rib cage had to be carried over the river and through the woods to the car. I was reminded how a gift can reciprocate to the giver in delightfully unpredictable ways.

# Dog Bed

Last night I shared my bed with a chihuahua, a mini-dachshund, an orange cat, and my husband. All of them snuggled in whatever comfortable crevice my legs and arms formed. Not wanting to disturb their sleep, I was afraid to change position. Today my limbs are stiff and my eyelids heavy, but the overwhelming feeling of mothering lingers.

Animals draw out the tenderness and the softness we falsely believe is a weakness. It is precisely our sense of security and protection that animals feel when we openly express our gentleness. Gentleness is a lighter shade of love's power, a power of love that is often underestimated.

Life is fragile. Without love to hold it together, the pieces fall apart.

## COYOTE CHICKEN

A little after midnight this morning, I was awakened by
two sharp yelps. My first thought was fox! Second thought,
chickens! I sent Wally out to run it off. Twenty minutes later he
was at the porch door waiting to come inside. Up to bed we
went. I opened my bedroom window just enough to listen to
the night's conversations. All of a sudden I heard a frenzy of
loud, excited howling and yelping, and then barking erupted.
It was answered by the sharp call I'd heard earlier. Coyotes! I
believe they were celebrating a catch. There were probably six
or so in the front woods.

The din went on for the time it took Wally to run up then
down a flight of stairs twice, with a slight pause at the landing to
whine. Andy was up now, and Wally was in full protection mode.

A quick decision was made to go check on the chickens.
I assumed Andy would be the one to go. He got out of bed,
went to the bathroom, found the flashlight, handed it to
me, and said, "You better put a coat on." Humph. "Wally will
protect you," he added.

I tramped out to the coop with my dim light and looked
back to see Wally on the porch, hairs extended like a Mohawk
from his neck to the tip of his tail, barking with a purpose and
with no intention of following me into the darkness.

I found the chickens roosting in the coop. All were accounted for and safe. As I finished, an owl let out a chorus of hoots five feet behind me, scaring the bajeebers out of me! I was beyond awake now and went over to give the horses some hay to calm them down.

I can listen to the coyotes howl all night when we go camping up north, but having to go out and face them close to home is an entirely different level of wild. I guess Wally showed me that courage can be on a sliding scale commensurate with the intensity of our fear. Fear at a distance and fear up close are two different perspectives of the same animal. As Franklin Delano Roosevelt said, "The only thing we have to fear is fear itself." Then what is a person to do if fear is what you fear most of all?

My solution is to put on your big-girl panties and go out to count the chickens.

## BEE HAPPY

For being a particularly good dog, Wally was treated to a leisurely walk around the farmstead. A jaunt to the farmstead is like taking him to Doggy Disneyland: rabbits, mice, pigeons, oh my! While there, we took time to meander our way to the beehive, following the sodden path that hugged the edge of the hay field. The walk was doing me good, clearing the gray out of the day. The sun wanted to shine, but the clouds were in the way. The air held the last of winter's cold breath and offered it back to the day in a misty breeze that stroked my cheeks with pleasant rouge.

On arriving, I was surprised to see the bees active. The scene felt surreal, with honeybee after honeybee zooming into the chilly air. The mesmerizing sight of these tiny beacons of summer-in-flight awoke my internal spring! Part your cloudy thinking and the sun will find a place to peek through.

# WALK IN BEAUTY

Walking Wally this morning, the gorgeous landscape pulled us around the edge of our neighbor's eighty acres as well our forty acres. Meditating on my feet has become a daily occurrence and something my sluggish body craved. At first, we poked along the rough stretch of ground. As the pace gained tempo, I felt an immense sense of gratitude for the agility my lower appendages offered up against the difficult portion of our journey.

I haven't acknowledged or given much attention to my legs in quite some time. These generous providers of miraculous movement tend to be taken for granted. It's astonishing how little effort it takes to put one foot in front of the other. Not only can I walk, but I can easily manage a brisk walk on uneven terrain over a distance of several miles with nary a moment's rest to catch my breath.

How would your life change if you couldn't walk? Every now and again, it's good to spend some time thinking about plain everyday things we take for granted. I love you short, currently hairy, legs! I love you crooked chubby toes! I love you bunions protruding from the side of each foot! Your beauty moves me.

# PART FIVE

# GOOD PEOPLE

## Soul Water

*I water you, you water me; we grow together.*
— Brandon Nembhard

The other day, while watering my potted plants, I noticed that if the soil in the pots goes for an extended period without water, it takes time for water to be absorbed. The water I pour in remains on the surface until the hard soil finally allows it to seep down to the roots. Even then, most of the water will run through. I have to return to water them again and sometimes a third time until the water is accepted by the roots. Only then can the parched plants quench their thirst.

I know some people who are like my parched potted plants. They've forgotten how to soak in life's juicy joy because they've lived so long with a closed heart. Angry and bitter, their spirits wither away, waiting for someone to pour love on them so they can soak in life.

Water a friend today.

# Wiggly Wig

Yesterday between bus routes, I buzzed into the local grocery store, Super Ron's, for a few quick things. But this often winds up being a forty-five minute adventure; I meet teachers from years past, bump into old classmates, or strike up the most interesting conversations with strangers.

Yesterday as I walked into the store, an elderly lady dropped her grocery list. I got my cart, then noticed that she couldn't bend down far enough to grab the rascally piece of paper. I picked it up and handed it to her after chasing it around the entranceway. I then asked politely if I could straighten her hair. Her wig had gone sideways on her when her efforts to bend down for the paper failed.

She asked politely if I could find a pen in her purse. We exchanged lighthearted words as I dug deep. Each item I pulled out had a story that she eagerly told me. My . . . our . . . frustration turned to giggles at the difficulty of this simple task. She flooded me with kind words of thankful appreciation and ended by saying, "I hope someone does something kind for you today."

I responded by saying, "They already have."

## LOVE'S STITCHES

I just finished stitching up my son Peter's favorite stuffed animal: a brown moose. He's traveled everywhere with us and is a bit tattered. Still, he's holding together just fine with the love of a little boy. With every stitch I felt love. Sometimes all we need are a few stitches of love to make us as good as new. I wish more people wanted to learn to sew. It teaches us that people shouldn't be so easily tossed away because they have a few holes in them.

# CHARLIE TREE

*Isn't there anyone who knows what Christmas is all about?*
— Charlie Brown

Before I join Andy outside, I've decided to enjoy a few more moments looking at our Christmas tree while sipping a freshly perked cup of coffee. I am keeping company with the melancholy that lingers, given the sweet memories of my dad that rest in my thoughts. Dad would have been out on the Oliver tractor pushing snow around by now.

I can still vividly remember planting Christmas trees with Dad over twenty-five years ago on a wet spring day. With great care, I gently pushed each of the baby tree roots into the narrow slot in the soggy earth. Dad made the slots with a tree spade he fabricated from the iron inventory kept next to the shed. Every so often we would stop to "take a five." Then he'd spit in his palms, grip the cold iron handle, and repeat the arduous task three hundred more times.

The tiny tree seedlings grew tall and proud. They have lived long past their prime years as Christmas trees, but it hasn't stopped us from fulfilling their purpose. We cut the top twelve feet from the overgrown trees to use as our Christmas trees. It might look "Charlie Brownish" to some, but I see the love that a father planted in his child, giving it room enough to grow.

# Anonymous Zucchini

What to do with all these lush rugged beauties? I sit contemplating zucchini's unappreciated wisdom. Since the middle of June, its presence has graced our family meals two or three times a week either as a hearty main dish, a simple side, or a sweet finale to a satisfying meal. Famously prolific, zucchini is versatile and grows successfully in a wide range of soils. My relationship with zucchini, however, changed this summer when I almost lost all my plants to a voracious infestation of squash bugs!

Bright yellow, bugle-shaped blossoms sound the arrival of the harvest. Zucchini is relentless in its obsession to propagate. Ripeness is a good night's sleep away. No time like the present to eat zucchini. Its flavor is delicate, some would say bland. I see zucchini as anonymous. It enhances any dish and tests the culinary creativity of backyard gardeners everywhere.

I aimed a long, fixed stare at its midnight-green skin, thick twisted stem, and smooth cylindrical body. Zucchini's wisdom is to know that ripeness exists in every moment. Be versatile. Get imaginative. Grow no matter what circumstances present themselves. The most genuine and generous giving is when the donor remains . . . anonymous.

Every once in a while it feels nice to be recognized for what you bring to life's plate, set on the table overlooking all of creation.

With a heart full of gratitude, I thank you, zucchini!

## CROWDED CORNER

The world needs variety in every walk of life. Opposite forces keep her spinning. I like dirt under my fingernails, though a lot of folks don't. I like to be outside, a lot of folks don't. I'm grateful for all the folks who aren't like me. Together we balance each other.

Instead of judgment, hold gratitude for difference. Having an appreciation for all that I am also means that I must have an equal appreciation for all that I am not.

# Zesty Apples

*Bean finds the best apple in our tree and hands it up to me. "You*
*know what this tastes like when you first bite into it?" she asks.*
*"No, what?"*
*"Blue sky."*
*"You're zoomed."*
*"You ever eat blue sky?"*
*"No," I admit.*
*"Try it sometime," she says. "It's apple-flavored."*
— Rodman Philbrick, *The Last Book in the Universe*

My Zest Star apples picked from our orchard brought me
a delicious taste of nostalgia. Apples were abundant in
my childhood. I looked forward to the sweet perfume and
cheerfulness of the spring blossom. I doubt many kids these
days have ever gotten a good bruising from a green apple fight.
First bruise was from the apples, second one was from Mom's
tongue, yelling at us for bruising perfectly good apples. The
apples not fit for human consumption were raked under the
electric fence for the cows.

I peeled apples for sauce and pies until blisters emerged
in defiance of the constant pressure of the peeler on my index
finger. Dad carried apples in his pocket, his truck, and his heart.

I fondly remember going with him to the homestead farm where he grew up to pick Wolf River apples from the old tree standing in the peaceful orchard. Wolf River apples grow to the size of softballs. Dad would drive the truck close in to the tree trunk, and I would climb on the cab roof to pick the best ones, bouncing in the sun on the highest limbs.

When apples rounded the top of the pail we would sit on the tailgate and prepare for a taste test. Dad would take his jackknife out, wipe the blade on his shirt sleeve, and slice off a wedge from a few choice apples.

The tree still grows but no longer bears fruit. I pass it daily on my school route. As I ripen with age, I know my wistful affection for the past is a good place to visit but not dwell. Still, I long for a taste of the past to be with me here and now. The solution is to extend a branch from the past into the present. A Wolf River apple tree will be planted in our orchard next spring to ensure that the memories rooted in the past can produce sweet fruits for future generations in our family tree.

# Finding Missing Pieces

*Appreciation is the highest form of prayer, for it acknowledges the presence of good wherever you shine the light of your thankful thoughts.* — Alan Cohen

Farming grew a taproot of reliability and dependability straight down the center of who I am. As a farmer, every day, whether you know it or not, something or someone depends upon you and values your place in this world. Growing up, appreciation for the most part was unspoken. You had to feel the worth of your actions because nobody was going to tell you.

Last weekend I gained a new perspective on how much Dad must have appreciated me being with him on the tractor to hook and unhook farm equipment. Finishing the field work alone, it took enough trips up and down the tractor steps that my knees started to protest. What I wouldn't have given for an eight-year-old kid to come trotting down the field lane.

The end of this school year marks my sixth year without missing a day of work. If you love what you do, you never work a day in your life, as they say. I have a new phrase for work: "a pleasurable pursuit of your purpose." I love what I do mostly because I feel appreciated. In this morning's mail, I was pleasantly surprised to receive a letter of appreciation from the

Sexual Assault Center for being the Most Reliable Volunteer.
It's these pieces of appreciation scattered over a lifetime that
piece together one's worth.

## Underlining Love

I love my mother-in-law, Marilyn Haen! She sends us a card
for every occasion, but what I love most is that in the card,
she underlines words that she wants to emphasize, those
that express what her heart wants to say. We received her
Valentine's Day card today. She underlined the following words:
loved, every, day, of the year, wished, ever, happiness, today,
always, Happy, Valentines, and Day! She underlined the entire
card, bless her heart. Obviously, words carry meaning. Marilyn
wants us to feel the words, not just read them. I love my
mother-in-law, and I wish I could underline her.

## Berry Sweet Friends

By late summer the ruby red clusters of Viburnum berries can be seen everywhere. The birds leave these beauties dangling because the berries are bitter until winter passes over them; they grow sweet with time. The peak of their sweetness comes in late spring when most of the winter food sources have been exhausted. Migrating Cedar Waxwings will gobble them up in a day or two.

In my life, I've waited for time to sweeten a few people who held bitterness in their heart. Trouble is, some couldn't let their winters pass over them, only through. Their hearts stayed frozen. They chose to remain sour. Sadly, the world is unable to taste their sweetness. Others have been able to face the harshness of cold truth and allow themselves to fully ripen. They are bursting with plump, juicy life.

To all my delicious friends and family who have gone through a winter or two, thank you for sweetening my journey.

## CHRISTMAS WISH

My Christmas wish this season: I pray we "peace" together
our world, patch up our differences, stitch joy around all its
seams, wrap each heart in a blanket of love, and feel with every
thread of our being the oneness that holds all souls together
for infinity.

## NAKED TRUTH

Well, Andy did it again. He managed to get everyone in the
family down to their skivvies, including me, with his first fire of
the season in the wood stove. Ugh! I asked him why he doesn't
learn from past years and not burn it so hot. His answer,
"Maybe I want to see you in your skivvies" (playful smile . . .
slight head tilt). "Did you ever think of that?" I guess that
means I'm finally seeing the naked truth with a slightly blushed
complexion. I am reminded of this quote by Benjamin Disraeli:
"Never apologize for showing feeling. When you do so, you
apologize for the truth."

## Colors of Karla

Sometimes you have to lose to win.
Empty to be full.
Look with your eyes closed.
Believe without seeing.
Tear apart to make whole.
Be sick to heal.
Imagine what is real.
Color yourself with your true colors there outside the lines you
drew.

# Plant Seeds

We rent our farmland to an organic farmer. He has struggled
with health issues, and although he makes an effort, he has yet
to harvest anything from our land. Last fall, barley seeds were
set in the soil very late in the growing season. There wasn't
enough of a crop to justify the use of harvesting equipment,
so the harvest was left standing in the field. This morning I
noticed the abundance of birds, rabbits, mice, and the like that
are finding nourishment and sustenance among the remnant
barley stalks and weeds. The impromptu habitat has in turn
attracted hawks and foxes. Even if we are unable to gather our
harvest, others will come along and garner nourishment.

At the end of your life, you want to look back and know
that you didn't leave a single regrettable seed unsown. I agree
with Henry David Thoreau: "The true harvest of my life is
intangible."

# Apples and Pears

We joined our daughter Sophie and a counselor for career planning. Sophie completed several personality/interest tests to pinpoint a career path for herself. She will do these tests all over again sophomore year. Andy and I suspect she is a left-brainer. A career heavy on logical thinking, like that of an accountant or actuary, would suit her best.

On one particular pie chart I noticed an "Animal/Plant" section. One dot meant little interest, two dots moderate, and three dots high interest. She didn't even have a dot . . . nothing . . . nadda . . . zero interest. I look at Sophie, mouth gaping open as I pointed to the pie slice. She giggled.

I've known for many years that our interests differ, yet we still manage to have a close relationship. I've learned so much by looking at things from her perspective.

From the moment they are born, we celebrate our children's similarities to us. But what to do when the apple falls far from the tree? I confess that part of me wanted my daughter to be a "mini-me." The other part of me knew it was better for her to find her own identity. Thus, I must trust that the good characteristics we instilled in her will take hold and become ingrained in the fiber of who she becomes through the growing process. Although she is on a different path, it is no better or worse than mine. She is a good person and that's all I've ever wanted my children to grow up to be.

# PART SIX

# HAIKU AND A TANKA

## Honey Haiku

Thick drop of honey —
What flower do you taste of
All of them at once.

## Joy Haiku

To the world give joy.
Around and around it goes.
From the world take joy.

## Green Ribbons Haiku

Green ribbons of grass,
Swaying to the wind's music.
May I have this dance?

## Free Heart Haiku

Rattle the caged heart.
Bend the iron bars of fear.
Free the world to love.

## Storm Haiku

Discharge your anger,
Quick as lightening to the earth.
And the thunder rolls.

## Tree Haiku

Stand in your tree truth.
Oak wise, pine soft, maple sweet.
In you, lives the tree.

## Lazy Rain Tanka

A lazy rain falls,
Soft sounds of sorrow and joy,
Play with my still thoughts.
Before going further down,
And this one slow drop sinks deep.

# PART SEVEN

# A LITTLE BIT DEEPER

# I Am Old Ground

I am old ground.

An earth child of sufficient depth, good tilth, and slope.
Birthed from the star nation eons ago, there exists in me
a mingling of stone wisdom and star vision,
I am old ground.

My prayers are silent twinkles. Simply there.
Like the feeling when you look out over a fallow field. Listening
to the tiny world of those things that creep and crawl, jump
and chirp.
Watching the patches of daisies play hide-and-seek among
slender ribbons of grass.
These are the rosary beads of life.
Notice the twinkles.
I am old ground.

Aging has slowed my body, ripened my mind, and sweetened
my Spirit.
Gifts I am grateful to be present to receive.
We are living graves, holes from heaven.
May I be shoveled full of love before I leave this world.
I am old ground.

Rich
Soft
Organic
Holy.

## Loose Reins

Gently, I slide a leg over my good little mare's bare back.
Leather reins in hand, a kiss and a cluck to ask her to move out.
Trust is a powerful muscle to flex. Horse and human invisibly
bonded.
Together equal practitioners of honest communication.
Our thoughts touching as intimately as our bodies.
The more I loosen the reins, the closer the ties.
Two hearts open wide and deep.
From here the throb of the earth's pulse echoes in my veins.
Hoof and heart beat as one.
From here her breath gives me life.
Horses run in my blood like oxygen.
Intuitively, she reads my body language as I read hers. I listen
with her, not for her. Feeling fear come and fear go.
Even though we travel the same trail, time and time again, it
isn't the same.
Is the sky a tinge bluer? Am I no longer a gangly, carefree
teenager?

I keep my focus on what matters, which is here and now. Reminding myself to loosen the reins. Trust that from here, I can go anywhere. Trail or no trail. The soul loves the freedom to connect. I let go of the reins. Happy stays on the trail. Joy comes home with you. Something I learned from gently sliding a leg over the bare back of my good little mare and asking her to move out with a kiss and a cluck.

# Fire Line

As this good day rises from under the cover of darkness,
the sky's face is hidden behind a soft gray veil.
Tree leaves in all shades of orange, yellow, and red
press tender kisses of color against the horizon.
A fine mist sifts through the air.
Droplets of water pearls string together and drape over
spider webs. Giving them the appearance of delicate lace hankies.
The distant horizon is on fire, a line of fire created from fall's flame.
Tree branches spit and sizzle against the dull backdrop. A
forgotten fire is rekindled.
Where do I feel the burn?
I see gaps in the fire line where the wind has raked the
branches bare.
Opening a way through. I go there.
A flame within me extinguished.
What's there in the ashes?

# LIFE'S LIBRARY

For me nature opens the book of life.

Aliveness on every page.

Every illustration drawn by some mysterious Divine hand.

Where one story ends, two begin.

Nature invites you to read between the lines in life.

Read between the words in relationships.

Read the spaces between the letters.

Go off the page for meaning.

Read what is written on souls.

Nature asks you to explore those things words cannot describe.

What is unspoken.

The narrator in the green world is your imagination.

It's what makes stories come alive. Use yours.

Don't judge yourself by the cover the world has bound you to.

We are the "good" book.

A sacred text.

Don't be afraid to look inside.

# Wild Mustangs

Wild mustangs run with me
Hooves pound over the earth cloud
Jump into the fearless raging river
Wash away the bank's security
Wet my soul
Wild freedom cannot be stopped
Which dam Oh-flood waters shall break
That I may be free?
Wild mustangs run with me
Hooves pound over the earth cloud
Lone windswept pine, shelter me.
Weather the heart's storms.
Magnificent deep roots
Stealing downward toward dark earth
Rich in knowing, deep in love
Feed me. Anchor me. Strengthen me
Wild mustangs run with me
Hooves pound over the earth cloud
Lightning strikes against my soul
Thunderbirds soar above the stampede
Surging life-force energy
Pulses aliveness through open prairie of my heart.

Fiery cracks and crackles, fierce claps
Awakening the sleeping light
Hiding under cover of darkness
Wild mustangs run with me
Hooves pound over the earth cloud
No ropes from the past can hold me
I run mustang free.

# Now It's Here

In every ordinary day,

There are extraordinary moments.

There goes one now!

You can't go back to get them.

You can't see them coming.

They're here — now.

## Love Blooms

When I lay on the field's colored blanket
ask me about sacred romance
between bee and flower. What inner call to unity draws them
together.
Take to the sky. Find the flowers.
Return the gifts gathered in the brightest light,
to the sanctified hive's deepest dark.
Ask me what the black light knows.
Listen to what the bees say. The Creator's tiny helpers carry
good medicine.
We know the nectar is there, unseen; and life buzzes by,
there all along, the sweetness collected in the spirit of the flower.
I say what the bee says: love blooms.

## Blessing from the Wood

The gift of strength from the mighty Oak,
The gift of gratitude from the humble Willow,
The gift of healing from the sacred Cedar,
The gift of love from the giving Birch,
The gift of peace from the serene Pine,
The gift of wonder from the ancient Sequoias,
The gift of joy from the quaking Aspens,
Bless the standing people of the Woods.

## Heart Mind

A heart must possess an imagination.
How else could hope exist?
And a heart that imagines, certainly dreams.
If only a mind could love.

# Sacred Motion

All at once a swoosh of wind tips an outcrop of lily pads on end.
Dish plates standing to dry.
Each lays down on the water's surface.
Again.
All at once.
White pine boughs rise and fall on cue.
Forced by a current high above.
Heard not seen.
Repeating the breath in, the breath out.
Lungs of the Universe.
A sunset-tinted lake
gives those of us
lusting for its attention
a myriad of flirty winks.
Pink candy clouds hang on the last of the day's sweet light.
Night hungers,
swallows them whole.
An Eagle's vision travels through the water's body.
Catching a life. Releasing death.
Observing all this, I sense the wheel of life spinning further around,
everything in sacred motion.

# About the Author

Angeline Haen was raised on a small dairy farm in Sobieski, Wisconsin, where the love of the earth and all things of nature collected in her heart. Through her participation in the Native American community in her later years, she learned how to nurture a relationship with all that surrounds her.

A former electrical / instrumentation journeywoman and stay-at-home mom, she is currently employed as a school bus driver. She and her husband, Andy, steward a forty-five acre hobby farm and tend to the needs of four beehives.

An avid gardener, Angeline earned her Master Food Preserver certification in 2012. Presently, she is rehabilitating a rescue horse the family adopted in May of 2014. In the past, she has volunteered for the Sexual Assault Center of Family Services in Green Bay, Wisconsin, where she supported victims of sexual assault and abuse. She is actively involved in the lives of her two children, Sophie, who is seventeen, and Peter, who is fourteen.

www.ingramcontent.com/pod-product-compliance
Lightning Source LLC
Chambersburg PA
CBHW041923090426
42741CB00020B/3457